Looking After Grandpa

Written by Rose Kelbrick
Illustrated by Donna McKenna

Mom and her friend
went to town.
The children had to
look after Grandpa.

"Who can make the beds?"
asked Grandpa.
"We can,"
said the children.
The children made the beds.

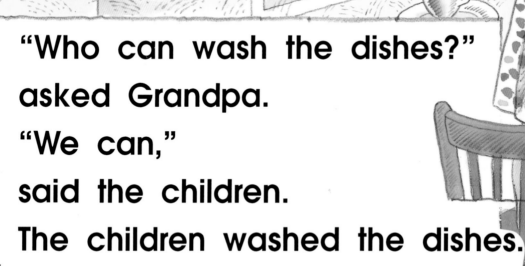

"Who can wash the dishes?"
asked Grandpa.
"We can,"
said the children.
The children washed the dishes.

"Who can clean the bathroom?"
asked Grandpa.
"We can,"
said the children.
The children cleaned the bathroom.

"The beds are made,
the dishes are washed,
the bathroom is clean,"
said Grandpa.

"Who can get the lunch?"
asked Grandpa.
"We can,"
said the children.